I0107557

"I AM FEARFULLY AND WONDERFULLY MADE" Psalm 139:14 EVERY DAY!

Sunday School Lessons to Build Self-Esteem in Children

"I AM FEARFULLY AND WONDERFULLY MADE" Psalm 139:14 EVERY DAY!

Sunday School Lessons to Build Self-Esteem in Children

MABEL ELIZABETH SINGLETARY

MightyWayBooks

©2017 by
MABEL ELIZABETH SINGLETARY

All rights reserved. No part of this book may be reproduced in any form without purchase and with the specific intention for use in a classroom setting or permission in writing from the publisher, except in the case of brief quotations embodied in critical articles or reviews.

Cover Art: DeepGreen
Illustrations: GN illustrator, gldcreations, ilonitta, JoJoStudio
Library of Congress, Washington, DC
Singletary, Mabel Elizabeth
    I Am Fearfully and Wonderfully Made Every Day! Psalm 139:14
Sunday school Lessons to Build Self-Esteem In Children

ISBN-13:978-0-9886553-4-8
ISBN-10:09886553-4-9

[1. Children—Non-fiction. 2. Faith—Non-fiction 3. Christian—Non-Fiction
4. God—Non-Fiction
5. Praise—Non-fiction 6.Self-esteem—Non-fiction. 7. African Americans—Non-fiction 8. Family Relationships—Non-fiction.]

All scripture quotations noted NIV are from the Holy Bible, New International Version.

MightyWayBooks.com

Mightywaybooks@gmail.com

Printed in the United States of America

This book is dedicated to the children of God in South Africa,
who, like all of God's children,
are "fearfully and wonderfully made".

"I praise you because I am fearfully and wonderfully made; your works are wonderful, I know that full well."

Psalm 139: 14, NIV

The scripture given above will be our starting point. It is taken from the inspired word of Almighty God. Psalm 139, verse 14 to be exact. It should serve as an anchor for every child of the Most High God no matter what the age or station in life. If we look to the Lord and allow His unconditional love to shower and cover us; when we look at our lives we will not just see the pain and devastation which can so easily rest itself in our minds, bodies, and souls. We can also see hope. Drawing closer to the One who created humanity, can allow us to see the reflection of God's love as it gently pours out into our hearts. Jesus allows us to see ourselves through the eyes of God. And when you look through Jesus' lens, you will see the child who was made with God's careful planning and intent; a child who was *"fearfully and wonderfully made"*. That truth alone gives each one of us reason to pause and give thanks and praise to the Lord our God. *Psalm 139:14* is a reminder that you have been created for a purpose. For some, this may be the start of your journey, while for others a continuation. It is the hope and prayer of the author that you will personally hear through the scriptures contained in this book, enjoy the stories and activities, and grow by leaps and bounds in your journey as a child of God.

Mabel Elizabeth Singletary

Table of Contents

January . . . . God's Love for You

February . . . . Trusting God

March . . . . Jesus Cares

April . . . . Joyfulness

May . . . . God's Word Gives Peace

June . . . . You Are Welcome!

July . . . . A Good Start

August . . . . I'm Special!

September . . . . Humility

October . . . . God My Protector

November . . . . Praise

December . . . . You're Part of God's Family!

January

Lesson Theme: God's Love for You

Opening Prayer:

Dear Lord,

Thank you for creating me in your image. Thank you for letting me know that I will always be special and important to you. In your word, you have said that "I am fearfully and wonderfully made." I praise you Jesus and thank you for your unconditional love today and every day of my life.

In Jesus name,

Amen.

Scripture: *"Children are a heritage from the Lord, offspring a reward from him. Like arrows in the hands of a warrior are children born in one's youth. Blessed is the man whose quiver is full of them . . ."* **Psalm 127:3-5**

Words to talk about: (Discuss vocabulary and give examples of these words used in context to help understanding.)

Heritage—something that is inherited or passed down.
Offspring—a person's child or children.
Reward—a prize or honor.
Blessed—having divine favor and protection.

Scripture Discussion:

Psalm 127:3-5 makes one thing very clear. ***God truly loves children***. According to the scripture, children are a "heritage from the Lord". You have been passed down from God and given as a reward from Him. God loves you every day. His love will never stop. Children are valuable and prized gifts from the Lord. God reminds us that those who have the responsibility of parenting children are blessed.

Story: **Seashells**

Pop Pop's eyes lit up with joy when his granddaughter Zama came into the room. He loved her very much. Sitting up in his chair, he looked at her and smiled. "It is good to see you Granddaughter!"

Zama returned Pop Pop's smile and gave him a big hug. "And I am glad to see you too," she said. Then she made him a warm cup of tea and they spent the afternoon talking about the fun they had when Zama was a little girl.

Pop Pop closed his eyes. "Do you remember when we collected those pretty seashells at the beach when you were ten?"

Zama laughed. "And do you remember how you told me to only take a few so there would be seashells for others to find?"

Pop Pop opened his eyes and looked at her. "I could tell you were a little sad about having to leave so many of your seashells behind."

"I was sad," said Zama. "But now I understand."

Pop looked surprised. "You do?"

"Yes," Zama said. "If I had taken all those seashells that day, we probably wouldn't have gone back so many other times like we did."

"And we did have fun. Didn't we Zama?"

"So much fun that one day I will tell my children about the great times I spent at the beach with my wonderful grandfather."

"You mean like the way I tell everyone about the times I have spent with my beautiful granddaughter?"

Zama smiled and touched her grandfather's hand. "I love you Pop Pop." Then reaching into her pocket, she took out a seashell and placed it in his hand. "I still have those seashells Pop Pop. Each one reminds me of you."

Questions:
1. Is Zama an example of a heritage? Explain.
2. Do you think Zama felt loved by her grandfather? Explain.
3. Give an example from the story that shows Zama felt valued.
4. Who makes you feel valuable? Explain why you feel this way.

Small Group Activity: (Provide students with poster boards, pencils, crayons, markers, old magazines, scissors, and glue.)

1. Create a poster of positive messages sent to you from God (You may use words, pictures, or a combination of both.)
2. Share your poster.
3. *(Optional) Display posters in classroom.

Writing:
Use the words below to finish the following sentences.

1. God says I am a _____ from Him.

2. Children are seen as a _____ in the eyes of God.

3. _____ means to have divine favor and protection.

4. An _____ is someone's child or children.

Blessed   Heritage   Offspring   Reward

God's Children Are . . .

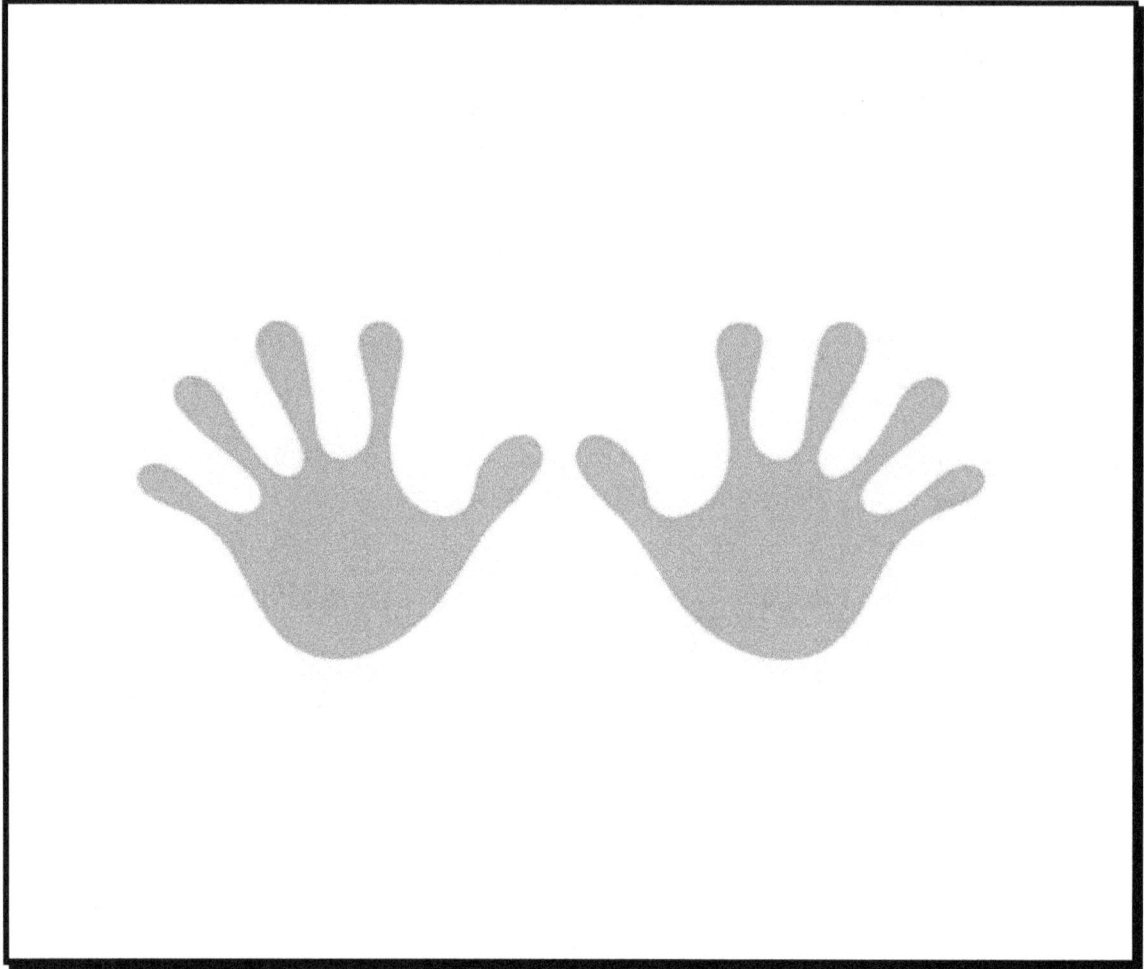

Write ten words in the box above from the list describing how God sees you.

Beautiful Smart Intelligent Talented Kind Happy Loved Good Handsome Pretty Gifted Helpful Friendly Special Important Caring Creative

Song: Encourage children to sing along as you teach the words to the song *"Jesus Loves Me"*.

Jesus Loves Me
By Anna B. Warner

Jesus loves me! This I know,
For the Bible tells me so;
Little ones to Him belong;
They are weak, but He is strong.

Chorus
Yes, Jesus loves me!
Yes, Jesus loves me!
Yes, Jesus loves me!
The Bible tells me so.

Jesus loves me! This I know,
As He loved so long ago,
Taking children on His knee,
Saying, "Let them come to Me."

Jesus loves me still today,
Walking with me on my way,
Wanting as a friend to give
Light and love to all who live.

Jesus loves me! He who died
Heaven's gate to open wide;
He will wash away my sin,
Let His little child come in.

Jesus loves me! He will stay
Close beside me all the way;
Thou hast bled and died for me,
I will henceforth live for Thee.

*Offer the invitation to discipleship at the close of each lesson (p.86).

Closing Prayer:

Dear Heavenly Father,

      Thank you for loving me and blessing me every day. You are a kind and loving God who created me as a reward. I am a heritage from you and I am so glad you made me. Thank you for showing me how much I mean to you.

      In Jesus' name I pray.

      Amen

February
Lesson Theme: Trusting God

Opening Prayer:

Dear Lord,

Please help me to listen and learn from the people you have sent to teach me in my youth. Help me to be wise as I read and study your Word. I want to believe and have faith in Your Son Jesus. Prepare my heart so I can receive Jesus as my Savior.

In Jesus name,

Amen

Scripture: *"But as for you, continue in what you have learned and have become convinced of, because you know those from whom you learned it, and how from infancy you have known the Holy Scriptures, which are able to make you wise for salvation through faith in Christ Jesus."* **2Timothy 3:14-15**

Words to talk about: (Discuss vocabulary and give examples of these words used in context to help understanding.)

Holy Scriptures—God's written word

Salvation—being delivered from sin

Faith—trusting God completely

Christ Jesus—Son of God

Wise—having knowledge

Infancy—childhood or babyhood

Scripture Discussion: Timothy was raised by his mother Eunice and his grandmother Lois. They saw to it that from the time he was a young boy, they taught him the Holy Scriptures. They knew the importance of creating the best foundation for Timothy. By sharing God's Word with him, he would become wise and keep the Lord close to his heart. Timothy trusted in the teachings of his mother and grandmother. And he learned to trust in the Word of God.

Story: *Trusting Jesus*

Corey always wanted to make the soccer team. He had practiced all summer and believed he was ready. He attempted to try out the year before, but something happened to change his plan. He probably could play as well as any of the other boys who had come for the tryouts. However, when it was time to show what he could do, he remembered what one of the boys had said to him on the way to the practice field. "Why are you wasting your time trying out for the soccer team?" A boy asked him.

"I love playing soccer," Corey answered. "And I think I can make the team."

"Well," said the boy. "I've seen you play and I think you're pretty bad! You're wasting your time. The coach will never pick you!"

Corey didn't make the team that year because he never tried out. He made a terrible mistake and listened to the boy's negative message. Corey doubted his own ability. He no longer believed he could make the team.

But something changed one Sunday. Corey heard his pastor telling about a God who could do the impossible in our lives when we trust him. "Philippians 4:13 says 'I can do all things through Christ who strengthens me!' The pastor announced. "We all can!"

Corey believed what he heard that day and decided to trust Jesus. He had come back and this time no one was going to tell him he wasn't good enough to make the team. He also knew he wasn't alone. He had Jesus in his heart. And he knew Jesus could do anything—except fail.

Questions:
1. Why didn't Corey try out for the soccer team the first time?
2. What can you do if you receive a discouraging message?
3. Share a time when you have been discouraged? How did you feel?
4. How can Jesus help you when you hear negative messages?

Activity: (Distribute crayons and colored markers.)

Using a large sheet of mural sized poster paper, have children write their hopes and dreams for a future that God can help them achieve. When done, let children share what they have written. *If possible, display completed project in classroom.*

Writing:
Write one sentence telling how trusting God's Word can help you.

_____

_____

Take Away: Make copies of *I will Put My Trust in Jesus* hearts page for students to take home. Encourage students to complete, bring back, and share.

I will put my trust in Jesus!

*Write your name inside the heart and decorate around it (write words and add pictures).

*Offer the invitation to discipleship at the close of each lesson (p.86).

Closing Prayer:

Dear Lord,

   Thank you for showing me I can always trust in you. Your Word is "a lamp unto my feet and light unto my path". *(Psalm 119:105)* Just like Timothy, I will listen and learn of your Son Jesus and trust in Him all the days of my life.

   In Jesus' name,

   Amen

March

Lesson Theme: Jesus Cares

Opening Prayer:

Dear Heavenly Father,

    Thank you for reminding me that I am special to you and that you care for me. Thank you for listening to my prayers and making me feel welcome when I come to you. Please continue to speak to my heart and help me to become the person you created me to be.

    In Jesus' name I pray,

    Amen

Scripture: *"People were bringing little children to Jesus for him to place his hands on them, but the disciples rebuked them. When Jesus saw this, he was indignant. He said to them, 'Let the little children come to me, and do not hinder them, for the kingdom of God belongs to such as these. Truly I tell you, anyone who will not receive the kingdom of God like a little child will never enter it.' And he took the children in his arms, placed his hands on them and blessed them."*

                                                  Mark 10:13-16

Words to Talk About: (Discuss vocabulary and give examples of these words used in context to help understanding.)

    Caring — Concerned; thoughtful, loving

    Disciples — Followers and or helpers of Jesus

    Kingdom — Territory ruled by a king or queen

    Rebuked — Turned away

    Indignant — Annoyed; not pleased

    Hinder — Block or hold back

    Receive — To welcome or accept

Scripture Discussion:

      Our Lord Jesus always has time for children. He is never too busy to listen to your prayers. In Mark 10:13-16, the disciples tried to turn away the children who wanted to see Jesus. They thought Jesus had more important things to do. However, they were wrong. Jesus was not pleased with the actions of the disciples. He told them to let the children come to Him and not hold them back because God's Kingdom belongs to those who receive the Lord like children. Once the children came to Him, Jesus blessed them.

Story: *Superstar*

Khalil wanted to see his favorite group "Superstar" more than anything. The group's lead singer Bheka had grown up in Khalil's hometown and that made the upcoming concert extra special. So when he heard they were coming to town, Khalil stood in line at the theater for hours hoping to get a ticket. There were many others in line too. Even though Khalil was at the end of the line; he wasn't going to change his mind about getting a ticket.

Looking from the back of the line Khalil hoped he'd make it to the front. *Maybe if I had come earlier*, he thought, *then I'd be closer to the front of the line by now.*

Suddenly the slow but steady movement of the line came to an unexpected halt. A serious looking man spoke loudly. "I am sorry to say," he announced. "There are no more tickets available for the 'Superstar' concert."

From the second he heard the announcement, Khalil had disappointment written all over his face. And long after everyone else had gone, Khalil still waited. Just as he turned to leave, his favorite group emerged from a side door of the theater.

Khalil spotted Bheka right away. "Bheka!" He shouted. "Can I have your autograph?"

Before Khalil could get any closer, some of the members of the group circled around Bheka. "Bheka doesn't have time right now," they said.

Bheka could see how hurt Khalil felt by the remarks. "Let him come," Bheka said. Reaching into his pocket he pulled out something and gave it to Khalil.

"It's a backstage pass!" Khalil shouted. "Thank you Bheka! This is even better than a ticket!"

Bheka smiled. "It's the least I can do for one of my biggest fans. See you at the concert!"

Questions:

1. Why had Khalil waited in line so long?
2. How do you think Khalil felt when he heard all the tickets were gone? Explain.
3. How would you feel if someone you admired had no time for you? Explain.
4. Why do you think Bheka gave Khalil the backstage pass?

Activity:

Assign children parts and have them role play the events in *Mark 10:13-16*. Rotate the parts to allow all children to participate in this activity. When done, lead children to understand that Jesus will always welcome them. (Help children make a meaningful connection with the story "Superstar" and Mark 10:13-16.)

Song: Teach children words to the song, *Jesus Loves the Little Children*

by C. Herbert Woolston

Jesus loves the little children
All the children of the world
Red, brown, yellow
Black and white
They are precious in His sight.
Jesus loves the little children
of the world.

Jesus died for all the children
All the children of the world
Red, brown, yellow
Black and white
They are precious in His sight.
Jesus died for all the children
of the world.

Jesus rose for all the children
All the children of the world
Red, brown, yellow
Black and white
They are precious in His sight.
Jesus rose for all the children
of the world.

Writing: Directions: (provide pencils and lined paper) If you could ask Jesus a question, what would it be? Write your question. (When done, allow volunteers to share.)

*Offer the invitation to discipleship at the close of each lesson (p.86).

Closing Prayer:

Dear Lord,

   Thank you for showing me how much you care about children. Thank you for letting me know through your Word that no one can keep me from the love you have for me. Please come into my heart to stay. Just as you welcome me; I welcome you.

   In Jesus' name,
   Amen.

April
Lesson Theme: Joyfulness

Opening Prayer:

Dear Lord,

Thank you for your continued love. I want to live to please you Father so that you will have joy. Help me each day to be pleasing in your sight as I walk with you and trust in your Word.

In Jesus' name,
Amen

Scripture: *"I have no greater joy than to hear that my children are walking in the truth."*   ***3John 1:4***

Words to talk about: (Discuss vocabulary and give examples of these words used in context to help understanding.)

Greater— better, larger, bigger
Joy— happiness
Truth— that which is true; a fact
Confident—sure of; certain

Scripture Discussion: As believers and followers of Christ, we are children of God. The Apostle Paul described those who follow God's Word as children who were walking in truth. Those who live by God's word give joy to the Lord as well as joy to those who are leading them.

Story: *Father's Joy*

"Sarah, will you lead our Sunday school class in prayer today?" Mrs. Nelson asked.

Sarah was afraid because she knew everyone would be listening. Her father was the Pastor and she knew her teacher and classmates were expecting a powerful prayer. She was afraid they would be disappointed. She loved God, but she was very shy and hardly ever spoke during her Sunday school lessons. Sarah quietly answered. "Can you please ask someone else Mrs. Nelson? I am not ready."

"You are a good student of God's Word Sarah, and I believe you are ready."

Sarah got up from her seat and walked to the front of her class. As she came forth, she silently prayed that the Lord would give her the right words to say. She cleared her throat with a small cough. "Please bow your heads," she said. "Dear Father in Heaven, I believe in you and I believe in your Word. Help each of us here to bring you joy as we learn of you and live in the truth you have given us. Thank you for sending your Son Jesus as our Savior, and thank you for watching over us every day. In Jesus name we pray. Amen."

Mrs. Nelson gave Sarah a big hug. "That was a beautiful prayer Sarah. I am sure your Heavenly Father was blessed."

Sarah learned in Sunday school that God is joyful when we live in His truth and follow His Word. When she looked toward the door of her classroom, she saw her father, the Pastor beaming with joy. That day Sarah learned that our earthly fathers are also filled with joy when they see their children living the Word of God.

Questions:
1. Do you ever feel afraid when called upon to do something? Explain.
2. What makes you feel brave?
3. Do you know that God loves you? Explain.
4. Does God know that you love Him?" Explain.
5. Do you think attending Sunday school can help you feel more confident to share God's Word? Explain.

Full Group Activity:

Teach children the words to the song *I've Got the Joy In My Heart.*
(Optional: add actions while singing.)

I've Got the Joy in My Heart

By George W. Cooke

I've got the joy, joy, joy, joy down in my heart
Where?
Down in my heart!
Where?
Down in my heart!
I've got the joy, joy, joy, joy down in my heart
Down in my heart to stay

And I'm so happy
So very happy
I've got the love of Jesus in my heart
Down in my heart
And I'm so happy
So very happy
I've got the love of Jesus in my heart.

I've got the love of Jesus, love of Jesus
Down in my heart
Where?
Down in my heart!
Where?
Down in my heart!
I've got the love of Jesus, love of Jesus
Down in my heart
Where?
Down in my heart to stay.

And I'm so happy
So very happy
I've got the love of Jesus in my heart
And I'm so happy
So very happy
I've got the love of Jesus in my heart.

31

I've got the peace that passes understanding
Down in the depths of my heart!
Where?
Down in the depths of my heart!
Where?
Down in the depths of my heart!
I've got the peace that passes understanding
Down in the depths of my heart!
Down in my heart to stay

And I'm so happy
So very happy
I've got the love of Jesus in my heart
And I'm so happy
So very happy
I've got the love of Jesus in my heart.

And if the Devil doesn't like it
He can sit on a tack!
Ouch!
Sit on a tack!
Ouch!
Sit on a tack!
And if the Devil doesn't like it
He can sit on a tack!
Ouch!
Sit on a tack to stay!

And I'm so happy
So very happy
I've got the love of Jesus in my heart
And I'm so happy
So very happy
I've got the love of Jesus in my heart

*Make copies of the next page and distribute to students.

Writing:

Directions: (Provide pencils.) Let children make as many words as they can from the word *JOYFULNESS*. Time this exercise and let volunteers share the words they made when done. (Optional: Children may work in pairs.)

_____   _____   _____

_____   _____   _____

_____   _____   _____

_____   _____   _____

_____   _____   _____

_____   _____   _____

_____   _____   _____

*Offer the invitation to discipleship at the close of each lesson (p.86).

Closing Prayer:

Dear Jesus:

    Thank you for letting me know that I can pray, sing, write, and tell others about you. Thank you for letting me bring you joy as I seek to live your Word. Please continue to help me learn of you.

    In Jesus' name,

    Amen

May

Lesson Theme: God's Word Gives Peace

Opening Prayer:

Dear Heavenly Father,

    I pray that you would give me teachers who will help me learn of you and keep your Holy Word in my heart. I ask that you would give me peace in my heart and in my mind when I am asleep and when I am awake. Thank you for loving me every day.

    In Jesus' name I pray,

    Amen.

Scripture: *"All your children will be taught by the LORD, and great will be their peace."*   ***Isaiah 54:13***

Words to talk about: (Discuss vocabulary and give examples of these words used in context to help understanding.)

    Taught— to be trained; educated
    Lord— Jesus
    Great— huge; enormous
    Peace— calm; quiet

Scripture Discussion:

    God loves His children richly. It is a love so great that it can be felt on the inside and show itself in our behaviors on the outside. God's teachings can cause his love to overflow and allows us to have peace in our hearts and in our minds. That peace can help us share God's love with others.

Story: *Peace for Jabu*

Jabu had been tossing and turning most of the night. He couldn't sleep and he was afraid. No one was with him and he prayed morning would come quickly. Every sound in the night seemed four times louder than it would have been during the day. Suddenly he remembered a prayer his grandmother had taught him. The prayer was called The 23rd Psalm. He prayed out loud and listened to every word as though he was listening to his grandma's voice.

"The Lord is my shepherd, I lack nothing.
He makes me lie down in green pastures,
he leads me beside quiet waters,
he refreshes my soul.
He guides me along the right paths
for his name's sake.
Even though I walk
through the darkest valley,
I will fear no evil,
for you are with me;
your rod and your staff,
they comfort me.
You prepare a table before me
in the presence of my enemies.
You anoint my head with oil;
my cup overflows.
Surely your goodness and love will follow me
all the days of my life,
and I will dwell in the house of the Lord"

When Jabu finished the prayer, he remembered he was not alone. Jesus would always be with him. "Thank you Jesus," he said and quietly drifted off to sleep.

Questions:

1. What did Jabu learn from his grandmother?
2. Do you think remembering and saying the prayer helped Jabu? Explain.
3. How did Jabu feel after he finished saying the 23rd Psalm?
4. What do we learn about God from the 23rd Psalm?

Writing: Make copies of next page, distribute, and provide pencils and crayons. Write a prayer to the Lord asking him to give you peace and help you feel God's love. Color your picture and share your prayer when you have finished.

_____

_____

_____

_____

_____

_____

Activity: Invite children to play a game called, *"Jesus Says"*. (The rules to this game are similar to *Simon Says*, a popular game played by children in America). Teacher or leader acting as Jesus will instruct children to follow every action made (examples such as wiggling fingers, raising an arm, stamping a foot, turning around, etc.) Players are eliminated if they do an action that Jesus didn't say to do.) Once children have caught on; let volunteers act as the leader.

*Offer the invitation to discipleship at the close of each lesson (p.86).

Closing Prayer:

Dear Lord,

Thank you Father for teaching me that I can pray and know that you are always near. Please help me to remember the 23rd Psalm so I can say it knowing you will hear me. Let this prayer be a reminder that in Christ, I can have peace. Help me to listen and study your Word so I can be more like Jesus each and every day.

In Jesus' name,

Amen

June

Lesson Theme: You Are Welcome!

Opening Prayer:

Dear Lord,

Show me how to be kind to others and friendly to everyone I meet. Help me to be thoughtful and generous so that your light will shine brightly through me. I love you Jesus and thank you for loving me.

In Jesus' name I pray,

Amen.

Scripture: *"Whoever welcomes one of these little children in my name welcomes me; and whoever welcomes me does not welcome me but the one who sent me."*
Mark 9:37

Words to talk about: (Discuss vocabulary and give examples of these words used in context to help understanding.)

Welcome— wanted
Whoever— any person
Sent— directed

Scripture Discussion:

Jesus saw great value in children—value that may have been missed by many people. Children couldn't be used to bargain for power or places of importance where Jesus was concerned. He knew that those who treated children properly had goodness in their hearts. If children were welcomed in Jesus' name, Jesus knew not only was He welcomed, but also His Father who had sent Him.

Story: *Come Right In!*

Corrine and her twin sister Carla stood outside the second grade classroom door. Corrine was afraid to enter. It was her first day and she didn't know anyone. "Come Corrine. I will be with you." Carla said taking her by the hand. "You don't have to be afraid."

Corrine pulled her hand away. "No," she cried, "I don't know anyone in there!

Carla looked through the window and saw the teacher. "Look Corrine! I see the teacher and she has a kind smile. And the children are smiling too. They look like they're having fun."

Corrine looked carefully through the window. "She does look like a nice teacher and I do want to learn."

Carla put her hand on the doorknob. "So are you ready to go inside?"

"Will you come in with me?"

"Of course I will." Carla said laughing. "We are both in this classroom."

Carla opened the door and everyone looked at her and her sister. Corrine stood right next to her.

"Welcome to second grade!" The teacher said greeting them warmly. "Come right in!"

"Welcome to second grade!" The children cheered.

Carla and Corrine stepped inside and both were wearing great big smiles.

Questions:
1. Why was Corrine afraid to enter the classroom?
2. What do you do when you feel afraid? Explain why this helps.
3. How do you think Carla knew the classroom was a good place to be?
4. Did Corrine feel differently once she stepped inside the classroom? Explain.

Full Group Activity: Teach students the song, *"Oh How I Love Jesus"*.

Oh How I Love Jesus
By Frederick Whitfield (1855)

There is a Name I love to hear,
I love to sing its worth;
It sounds like music in my ear,
The sweetest Name on earth.

Refrain:
Oh, how I love Jesus,
Oh, how I love Jesus,
Oh, how I love Jesus,
Because He first loved me!

It tells me of a Savior's love,
Who died to set me free;
It tells me of His precious blood,
The sinner's perfect plea.

It tells me of a Father's smile
Beaming upon His child;
It cheers me through this little while,
Through desert, waste, and wild.

It tells me what my Father hath
In store for every day,
And though I tread a darksome path,
Yields sunshine all the way.

It tells of One whose loving heart
Can feel my deepest woe;
Who in each sorrow bears a part
That none can bear below.

It bids my trembling heart rejoice;
It dries each rising tear;
It tells me, in a "still small voice,"
To trust and never fear.

Jesus, the Name I love so well,
The Name I love to hear:
No saint on earth its worth can tell,
No heart conceive how dear.

This Name shall shed its fragrance still
A long this thorny road,
Shall sweetly smooth the rugged hill
That leads me up to God.

And there with all the blood-bought throng,
From sin and sorrow free,
I'll sing the new eternal song
Of Jesus' love for me.

Writing: Copy and distribute the following page to each child. Fold the page in half. Have them color and decorate the cover. Draw a picture and write a welcome message to Jesus inside. Share your card when completed.

Dear

Jesus . . .

*Offer the invitation to discipleship at the close of each lesson (p.86).

Closing Prayer:

Dear Lord Jesus,

    Thank you for making me feel welcomed in your presence. Thank you for helping me learn how to pray for myself and others. I need you and I am so very glad that you are always near. I welcome you into my heart and ask that you will lead me and guide me every day of my life.

    In Jesus' name,

    Amen

July
Lesson Theme: A Good Start

Opening Prayer:

Dear Heavenly Father,

Thank you for those who pray for me each day. Help me to carefully listen and learn of you. I want to know you and follow you all of my life. Thank you for coming down from Heaven to save me.

In Jesus' Name I pray,

Amen.

Scripture: *"Start children off on the way they should go, and even when they are old they will not turn from it."*   **Proverbs 22:6**

Words to talk about: (Discuss vocabulary and give examples of these words used in context to help understanding.)

Start—beginning; birth
Way—pathway; direction
Turn—bend; change direction
Mercy—kindness; compassion; forgiveness

Scripture Discussion:

God wants to get to know you better right at the beginning of your life, and He wants every child to start off on the right path. God knows when you are taught about His love and mercy at a young age, you will be more likely to embrace His love and share the kindness, compassion, and forgiveness you have received from His teachings.

Story: *Pretty Pillows*

Amahle observed her grandmother as she carefully sewed the last stitch on the beautiful pillow she had made. For many years people in the community bought the decorative pillows from her. Amahle was so proud of her grandmother's special talent. "It's so pretty Grandmother!"

Grandmother smiled. "Come near Amahle so you can see and learn how to sew like me."

Grandmother handed a large sewing needle and a piece of material to Amahle. She had threaded the needle with pretty pink yarn. "Now," Grandmother said. "Watch and do exactly what I do." Grandmother stuck the needle into the material on one side and brought it out on the other side. She did the same thing again. And then she looked at Amahle. "I want you to try."

Amahle took the needle with the pink thread and guided it into the material and brought it out just as Grandmother had done. "Is it right Grandmother? Did I sew correctly?"

Grandmother examined the stitch Amahle had made in the material. "Yes," she said. "We will continue. Please watch me carefully so you can learn to sew."

"How did you learn to make such pretty pillows Grandmother?"

Grandmother smiled. "My grandmother taught me. She told me if I learned to stitch properly as a young girl, I would remember how to do this when I became an adult."

"Will I be able to make beautiful pillows someday like you Grandmother?"

"If you practice and learn from me, you will one day make pretty pillows of your own."

"Then I want to learn," said Amahle. "And one day I will teach my granddaughter how to make pretty pillows too."

Questions:

1. What talent did Amahle's grandmother possess?
2. Why did Grandmother want Amahle to watch her?
3. Do you think Amahle will continue her sewing when she grows up? Explain.
4. What have you learned that you would like to pass on to someone? Explain.

(*Make copies of the next page and distribute to students.)

Activity: *Find the words listed in the puzzle. Hint: Proverbs 22:6

and are beginning children compassion even forgiveness
from kindness love mercy not off old path right should
start the they turn way when will

A Good Start

```
h g n h w f n r d c c c z r v
p b o b y c v r l l u d n a k
h e k z z n o t u c u l o v e
g g e t r v h m h t t o s i k
g i m b j g f i p o h w h n t
n n l l i w l i n a a e w s r
e n n r h d i a g y s h y u a
v i f o r g i v e n e s s c t
e n f e m o s s e n d n i k s
n g n q o i f t d q t e n o h
z r e e r e h f l a h x r y n
d n l q f t r m o d e c w a c
s g a e a e e o z w w g p y b
y i x p d a g p q t l i w f y
m e r c y f l e i u s l j b w
```

50

Writing: (Make copies of this page and distribute to students.) *Draw a line to match each word to a synonym (words which have the same meaning).

1. Way   a. beginning
2. Turn   b. correct
3. Mercy   c. direction
4. Start   d. route
5. Path   e. manner
6. Right   f. compassion

*Choose 3 words from the left column and write three sentences. Let volunteers share their sentences.

_____

_____

_____

_____

_____

_____

_____

*Offer the invitation to discipleship at the close of each lesson (p.86).

Closing Prayer:

Dear Lord,

     Thank you for letting me know that learning about you can start today. Thank you for sending people who love and care about me enough to share your Holy word. Please help me to stay on the right path so that even when I am old, I will never turn away from your word.

     In Jesus' name I pray,

     Amen

August

Lesson Theme: I'M Special!

Opening Prayer:

Dear Father God,

Thank you for reminding me how special I am to you. You took your time and carefully created me in your image. I can forever praise you for the wonderful works you have done.

In Jesus' name,
Amen

Scripture: *"For you created my inmost being; you knit me together in my mother's womb. I praise you because I am fearfully and wonderfully made; your works are wonderful, I know that full well."* **Psalm 139:13-14**

Words to talk about: (Discuss vocabulary and give examples of these words used in context to help understanding.)

> **Create**— make; form
> **Image**— copy; likeness; reflection
> **Praise**— worship; honor; devotion
> **Wonderful**— magnificent; pleasing
> **Inmost being**— deeply inside
> **Womb**— place in female body where baby is carried until birth

Scripture Discussion:

God's description of children is nothing short of amazing. That is how he sees you. He created you and watched you grow inside your mother's womb knowing that each person born is uniquely individual. God knows the exactness of your inner self. When we realize and understand the care the Lord has taken to create us; we should always be ready to offer Him praise.

Story: *Beautiful Inside Out*

Lindiwe studied the girl on the magazine cover then looked in the mirror. "Why don't I look like this girl?" She asked herself. "Why am I not pretty like her?"

Lindiwe's mother was passing by her room when she heard what her daughter said. "Oh my daughter you are so wrong." Her mother said gently putting her hands around Lindiwe's face. "When I look at you I see someone so beautiful and special. Do you not know that the same God who made the heavens, the stars, and the earth also made you?"

"But Mama, I do not feel special or beautiful. I don't look like this girl at all. She is on the cover of a magazine because someone thinks she is pretty."

"And you, my daughter, are on the cover of God's heart. Every child made by God is beautiful on the inside and on the outside too. Do you know why?"

Lindiwe shook her head. "No Mama."

"It is so because God says it is."

Mama reached for her Bible and turned to the very first book. It was called the book of Genesis. She began to read. 'So God created man in His own image; in the image of God He created him; male and female He created them' (Genesis 1:27). "I just read from Genesis; the first book of the Bible; God's Holy Word." Then Mama read some more. " 'Then God saw everything that He had made, and indeed it was very good.' " (Genesis 1:31)

Lindiwe put down the magazine and again looked at herself in the mirror. "If God says I am created in His image, then it is so. I am beautiful inside and outside because God is my Father and I am His child!"

"Yes you are," said Mama. "Yes you are."

Questions:
1. Why did Lindewe think she wasn't pretty?
2. Do you ever compare yourself to others? Explain.
3. Do you believe what God says about you? Explain.
4. Tell why you are special?

*Make copies of this page for writing activity.

Full Group Activity: Teach children the cheer below. Add hand gestures and steps to make the activity fun.

Lift your hands up to the sky!
Praise the Lord who sits on high!
He died for me; He died for you,
His love for us is surely true!

He makes us new from inside out,
And calls us His without a doubt.
We are His children; you and me,
His life He gave to set us free!

JESUS!

Writing:

*Finish the following statement: (***Encourage children to share their sentences when done.**)

Learning about Jesus makes me feel

_____

_____.

*Offer the invitation to discipleship at the close of each lesson (p.86).

Closing Prayer:

Dear Heavenly Father,

     I can feel good about myself because of you. You made me in your image and that means I am special. Thank you for loving and caring for your children. You are forever my God and my King. I love you.

     In Jesus' name,

     Amen.

September

Lesson Theme: Humility

Opening Prayer:

Dear Lord,

I am your child and I am so thankful for your unconditional love. Help me to be humble and live my life to show my love for you. Give me a heart that wants to help others. Please Father, I pray that you will always let people see your love through the acts of kindness you inspire me to do.

In Jesus' name,

Amen

Scripture: *"At that time the disciples came to Jesus and asked, 'Who, then, is the greatest in the kingdom of heaven?' He called a little child to him, and placed the child among them. And he said: 'Truly I tell you, unless you change and become like little children, you will never enter the kingdom of heaven."* **Matthew 18:1-3**

Words to talk about: (Discuss vocabulary and give examples of these words used in context to help understanding.)

Humility— to be modest; humble.

Greatest—best; highest.

Unconditional Love—God's love for people does not change. He loves saints and sinners.

Jesus—The living Son of God the Father. Jesus is God in human form.

Heaven— God's Kingdom; Paradise. Christ has prepared such a place for those who believe His Word.

Kingdom—The dwelling place of a king. God is our forever King. He is the designer of all creation.

Disciples— Committed followers of Jesus (past, present, and future).

Scripture Discussion:

The disciples wanted Jesus to tell them who was the best in God's Kingdom. In this scripture, Jesus uses a child as an example to illustrate the kind of attitude one must have to enter the Kingdom of God. The modesty and humility possessed by children is what gets God's attention. There is never a need to compete for a special place in God. He has freely opened the door for each and every person through His Son Jesus, and He lovingly invites all to come in.

Story: *There's Room for Everyone!*

Elizabeth grumbled and pushed past the other boys and girls. "Move out of my way!" She declared making her way to the front of the line.

A much smaller girl looked up at Elizabeth. "But we were already here. You should wait your turn."

"Yes," said a boy standing in line. "We have been waiting. Why should you be first?"

"I should be first because I'm special," Elizabeth boasted. I'm the smartest and I'm the prettiest of all the children standing here."

After hearing what Elizabeth said, a young boy came from the back of the line to where she was standing. "Yes," he said. "You are pretty, but so is she," he said pointing at another girl in line.

"And she is too," said another girl. "We just don't go around bragging about it."

A boy at the end of the line called out. "And we're all smart too!"

Elizabeth didn't look happy. "Who says you're all pretty and smart?"

The little girl standing next to Elizabeth grinned. "God says so; that's who. He also says we don't have to worry about being first all the time because God loves us all and His heart has enough room in it for everyone."

"Is God's heart big enough for me too?" Elizabeth asked.

The little girl smiled at Elizabeth. "Of course it is!"

"Then you're right," said Elizabeth. "I don't have to be first *all* the time."

What Elizabeth did next surprised everyone. She took her place at the end of the line.And all children who had been waiting applauded Elizabeth for doing what was right.

Questions:

1. Was Elizabeth's behavior an example of being humble? Explain.
2. What does it mean to be humble? Give an example.
3. Does God want us to think about and be considerate of others? Explain.
4. What behavior would be the opposite of being humble?
5. Tell how you feel when you do the right thing.

*Activity page: Make copies of page 63 and distribute to students. Provide pencils, crayons, and markers. Encourage students to share their pictures when done.

Directions: Draw and color a picture showing an act of kindness (examples of sharing with or caring for others). Share your picture when you are done.

*Make copies of this page and distribute to students. Provide pencils.

Writing: Finish the poem on the lines below. (Encourage children to share when done.)

I will be kind to everyone,
and let them see God's love.

_____

_____

_____

_____

_____

_____

Name_____

*Offer the invitation to discipleship at the close of each lesson (p.86).

Closing Prayer:

Dear Jesus,

Teach me how to be humble and show kindness and love to others. I want to be more like you Lord. Please let people see that you are living in me. I love you.

In Jesus' name,
Amen.

October

Lesson Theme: God My Protector

Opening Prayer:

Dear Lord,

Thank you for telling me in your Word how dear I am to you. As I walk with you each day, please help me make good choices. I want to be more like you in what I say and what I do. Thank you for blessing me with people who show kindness and who are examples of your love. Please keep me safe from harm and danger.

I love you Jesus.

In Your name I pray,

Amen.

Scripture: *"And whoever welcomes one such child in my name welcomes me. If anyone causes one of these little ones—those who believe in me—to stumble, it would be better for them to have a large millstone hung around their neck and to be drowned in the depths of the sea."* **Matthew 18:5-6**

Words to talk about: (Discuss vocabulary and give examples of these words used in context to help understanding.)

Stumble— fall
Millstone— load; weight
Drowned— go under; sank
Depths— lowest point; rock bottom

Scripture Discussion:

Every child is valuable in the eyes of God. The Lord sees those who treat children well as having done the same for Him. In Matthew 18-5-6, God not only expresses His love for children; He also gives a warning to those who get in the way of believers (children of God). The Lord says that those who cause His children "to stumble" would be better off drowned at the bottom of the sea with a great weight around his neck. Truly this scripture reminds us that the Lord watches over His children. He is our protector.

Story: *Protector*

The wind and rain blew hard against the small cottage. "I am afraid!" Gabisile cried. "I want it to stop!"

"Me too," little sister Sizani said whimpering and holding tightly on to Gabisile. Both girls shivered every time the wild mix of rain and wind struck the house.

Father and Mother tried to calm the children. "It will be alright," said Mother. "The storm should be over soon."

"Yes," Father said. "We don't have to worry. All will be fine."

Gabisile looked at her Father wishing she could be as brave as he. *How do Mother and Father know we will be alright?* She wondered. *And how can they be so sure about it?* Gabisile studied them both looking to see if her parents showed even a little fear.

All of a sudden, the cottage was hit so hard that the girls could feel it shaking. "Help us Mother! Help us Father!" They screamed.

Mother and Father knew they could not control the storm, but they knew someone who could protect them all. Father and Mother got on their knees and wrapped their arms around their children while Father prayed. "Oh Lord Jesus, please protect us from the storm outside. Just as you look after us when the sun is shining; we know you can keep us safe from the wind and the rain. Thank you for being here with us. Amen."

Gabisile and Sizani could still hear the storm, but realized it no longer sounded so loud and scary. "God heard your prayer Father! He is protecting us!" Gabisile said.

"Yes my daughter, the Lord hears every prayer and he loves and protects his children."

"Amen," said Mother.

"Amen," said the children.

Questions:
1. Why were the children so afraid?
2. Do you think Mother and Father were also afraid? Explain.
3. Why do you think Father prayed during the storm?
4. Do you think God hears your prayers? Explain.
5. Do you think God only hears your prayers when you're afraid? Explain.

*Make copies of page 69 and distribute to students to write a message to Jesus and color. Provide pencils, crayons, and markers.

Activity: Write a message to Jesus on the banner and color. Share your banner when done.

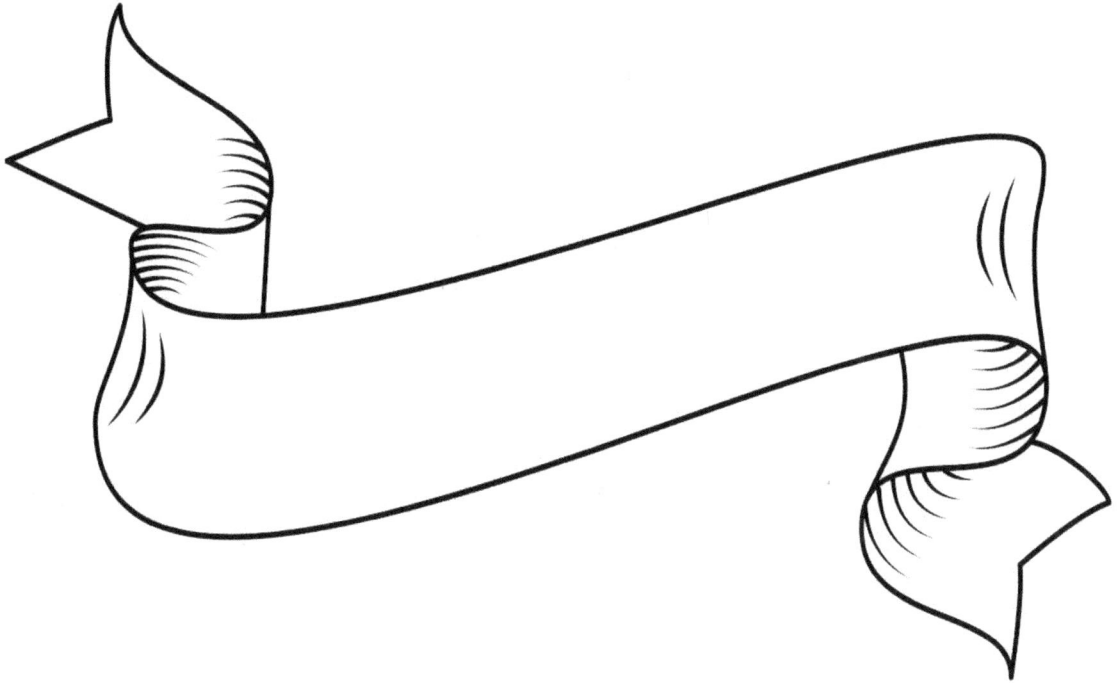

Name_____

*Teach song: *God is So Good*
By Velna A. Ledin

God is so good,
God is so good,
God is so good,
He's so good to me!

God answers prayer,
God answers prayer,
God answers prayer,
He's so good to me!

He cares for me,
He cares for me,
He cares for me,
He's so good to me!

I love Him so,
I love Him so,
I love Him so,
He's so good to me!

I'll do His will,
I'll do His will,
I'll do His will,
He's so good to me!

I praise His name,
I praise His name,
I praise His name,
He's so good to me!

*Make copies of next page and distribute to students. Share answers and sentences when done.

Writing: Circle the words that describe God as a protector. Choose four words and write one sentence for each word.

Brave   Hero   Listener   Afraid   Defender

Champion   Enemy   Guardian   Savior   Shield

Accuser   Foe   Guard   Friend   Helper

Opponent   Conqueror   Victor   Harmer   Warrior

Supporter   Advocate

_____

_____

_____

_____

_____

_____

*Offer the invitation to discipleship at the close of each lesson (p.86).

Closing Prayer:

Dear Jesus,

You are my Lord and my God. Thank you for protecting me. I know
that you welcome me and I appreciate those who treat me well and show
Godly love. I love you Jesus for loving me just as I am.

Thank you.

In Jesus' name,

Amen.

November

Lesson Theme: Praise

Opening Prayer:

Dear Lord,

I am so glad you are my Heavenly Father. Thank you for giving me a voice that I can use to sing, pray, and praise you every day. I know that when you hear my praise; it makes you smile. So I will praise you all of my days.

In Jesus' name,

Amen.

Scripture: *"Through the praise of children and infants you have established a stronghold against your enemies, to silence the foe and the avenger."*

Psalm 8:2

Words to talk about: (Discuss vocabulary and give examples of these words used in context to help understanding.)

Praise— worship; honor

Infants— babies

Established— formed; begun; created

Stronghold— sanctuary; fortress

Enemies— opponents

Silence— quiet

Foe— enemy

Avenger— vindicator; one who upholds

Scripture Discussion:

God has given His children a direct line to Him through prayer. He has also provided another way for everyone to reach Him and that is through praise. God's Word tells us that praise will act as a barrier that enemies will not be able to enter. Your praise is a direct line to the ears and heart of Almighty God. Giving praise to the Lord will silence enemies.

Story: *Let's Praise The Lord!*

Mrs. James was starting a children's choir at Bethany Church. She was so surprised to see the large number of children who had come to try out. As each child sang for Mrs. James she could feel the joy of their voices in her heart. "We will have a wonderful choir," she told the children. "Never have I heard such beautiful voices."

"Thank you Mrs. James," the children said.

Just as Mrs. James was about to dismiss everyone and give the next rehearsal date, a young girl came into the room. "I'm sorry for being late, but I hope I can still try out for the choir."

Mrs. James smiled. "Sure you can. There can never be too many voices singing and lifting praise to the Lord. Can you tell me your name please?"

"Yes, my name is Faith."

"And what a pretty name you have."

Mrs. James sat down at the piano. "Sing something you like and I'll join in."

Faith began singing the words to the song *'Jesus Loves Me'*. "Cause the Bible tells me so." She stopped singing because some of the children were laughing.

"She can't sing!" One child said. "How can she be in the choir?"

Faith was so embarrassed. She hung her head and started walking toward the door.

"Where are you going Faith?" Mrs. James asked. "Choir practice is not over."

"I can't sing very well, so I shouldn't be in the choir."

"That's not true. God wants every voice to praise him, and that praise begins in your heart. Praise can be singing, dancing, playing instruments, and so much more. Jesus loves to hear our praise. I want you to be in the choir and I want you to sing from your heart. If you do that, the joy you feel will come out as praise and flow into God's ears. Praise like that will always be in tune."

Questions:

1. Why do you think Faith came late to try out for the choir?
2. Do you allow others to discourage you from trying new things that may help you grow in your faith? Explain.
3. Did Mrs. James give Faith good advice about being in the choir? Explain.
4. Will Faith come back for the next rehearsal? Explain.

Full Group Activity: Teach children the words to the song:

Praise Him in the Morning

Author - unknown

Praise Him!
Praise Him!
Praise Him in the morning,
Praise Him in the noontime.
Praise Him!
Praise Him!
Praise Him when the sun goes down!

Love Him!
Love Him!
Love Him in the morning,
Love Him in the noontime.
Love Him!
Love Him!
Love Him when the sun goes down!

Serve Him!
Serve Him!
Serve Him in the morning,
Serve Him in the noontime.
Serve Him!
Serve Him!
Serve Him when the sun goes down!

*Make copies of the next page and distribute to students. Provide pencils. Encourage students to share their words when done.

Writing: Unscramble the words below. (*Hint: Use Psalm 8:2 and November's lesson vocabulary to help you solve for each word.)

1. ildchner _____

2. erapsi _____

3. gldooshrtn _____

4. stanifn _____

5. nmeeesi _____

6. oef _____

7. eenscil _____

*Offer the invitation to discipleship at the close of each lesson (p.86).

Closing Prayer:

Dear Lord,

    Thank you for blessing me with a voice that I can use to sing praises to you. Thank you for giving me hands to lift and clap as I praise your name. I know it makes you happy when you hear children giving you praise. I will praise you every day dear Jesus. I will praise you every day.

    In Jesus' name,

    Amen.

December

Lesson Theme: You're Part of God's Family!

Opening Prayer:

Dear Jesus,

Thank you for welcoming me into your family. I love you and invite you into my heart to stay. I know you are a loving and faithful Father. I feel warm and accepted in your presence. May I always praise you and live by your Word.

In Jesus' name I pray,
Amen.

Scripture: *"But as many as received Him, to them He gave the right to become children of God, to those who believe in His name."* ***John 1:12***

Words to talk about: (Discuss vocabulary and give examples of these words used in context to help understanding.)

Family— clan; lineage; kinfolk
Invite—request; offer
Faithful—truthful; committed
Right—claim; permission
Believe—accept; have faith in

Scripture Discussion:

Every person who accepts Jesus into his or her heart and believes Him to be the Son of God becomes a member of God's family. Being welcomed into and becoming a part of the family of God cannot be earned. It is a gift which is freely offered to all. Kinship with Christ happens at the very moment when an individual accepts the Lord's sacrifice of His life on the cross for all of mankind.

Story: *You Are Family*

When Michael came into the room, he wondered why his foster brother Trey looked so sad. A year ago Trey lost both his parents in a terrible accident and for the past ten months he's been living with Mr. and Mrs. Allen and their two children Michael and Stacy. He is grateful that they have opened their home to him, but Trey knows it is only temporary.

"What's wrong Trey?" Michael asked.

Trey thought about not answering, but Michael had really been nice to him—almost like a real brother. "I like it here," he answered.

Michael playfully tapped Trey on the back. "Then why are you looking like that?"

"Like what?"

"Like you don't have a friend in the world."

"I was thinking about how much I like being here with all of you. Mr. and Mrs. Allen have been so kind to me. They have treated me just like they treat you and Stacy. I am starting to feel like I love them and you guys—almost as if they were my parents too. I don't want to leave."

Neither Michael nor Trey saw Mr. and Mrs. Allen standing in the doorway. They heard everything the boys had said. When Mr. Allen coughed to clear his throat, the boys were surprised to see him and Mrs. Allen. "We feel the same way about you Trey."

"Yes," said Mrs. Allen. "You have become like one of our own children. And if you'll have us; then we would love to adopt you into our family."

Trey's sadness disappeared and was replaced instantly with joy. "Yes," he cried. "I would love to be part of your family!"

"You already are," Michael told him. "You already are."

Questions:

1. Why was Trey feeling so troubled?
2. Do you think Michael was a good foster brother? Explain.
3. How did Trey feel about the Allen family?
4. How do you think Stacy will feel about the adoption? Explain.

Activity: Teach the song; **I Have Decided to Follow Jesus** by S. Sundar Singh

I have decided to follow Jesus;
I have decided to follow Jesus;
I have decided to follow Jesus;
No turning back, no turning back.

The world behind me, the cross before me;
The world behind me, the cross before me;
The world behind me, the cross before me;
No turning back, no turning back.

Though none go with me, still I will follow;
Though none go with me, still I will follow;
Though none go with me, still I will follow;
No turning back, no turning back.

My cross I'll carry, till I see Jesus;
My cross I'll carry, till I see Jesus;
My cross I'll carry, till I see Jesus;
No turning back, no turning back.

Will you decide now to follow Jesus?
Will you decide now to follow Jesus
Will you decide now to follow Jesus?
No turning back, no turning back.

*Copy page 84 and distribute to students. Provide pencils.

Writing: Unscramble the message and write it on the line below. Have a volunteer read the unscrambled sentence aloud.

| INTO | BEEN |

| I | ADOPTED | GOD'S |

| FAMILY. |  | HAVE |

_____

_____

*Offer the invitation to discipleship at the close of each lesson (p.86).

Closing Prayer:

Dear Lord Jesus,

Thank you for adopting me into your family. I feel welcomed and honored. Thank you for being my Lord, my Savior, and my God. I will worship and praise you forever.

In Jesus' name,

Amen.

Prayer of Salvation

Dear Lord Jesus,

I confess that I am a sinner. I am sorry for my sins and ask for your forgiveness. I believe that you are the Son of God who came from Heaven, shed your blood and died on the cross as a sacrifice for me. I believe that on the third day you rose from the grave and are now seated at the right hand of God the Father in Heaven.

Jesus, I invite you to come into my heart and save my soul. Thank you for giving me eternal life.

In Jesus' name, I pray.

Amen.

". . . God has said, "Never will I leave you; never will I forsake you."

Hebrews 13:5 NIV

Answers

January

Questions:

1. Yes, she is a granddaughter.
2. Yes, he was glad to see her.
3. Grandfather enjoyed spending time with her.
4. Answers will vary.

Writing:

1. Heritage
2. Reward
3. Blessed
4. Offspring

February

Questions:

1. Another player said he wasn't good enough to make the team.
2. Remember how much God values children.
3. Answers will vary.
4. God's Word will encourage you (accept reasonable answers).

Writing:
Examples of acceptable answers: **making good decisions, being kind and showing respect to others, being trustworthy, having faith, compassion, integrity, being fair, and being humble**

March

Questions:

1. He wanted to see his favorite group perform.
2. Khalil was disappointed after having waited in line for hours.
3. Accept any answer indicating disappointment or hurt.
4. Bheka's fans were important to him.
5.

Writing:
*Let volunteers share their written questions.

April

Questions:

1. Accept answers which reflect an understanding of the question.
2. Answers will vary.
3. Accept reasonable answers and Refer students to 3John 1:4.
4. Accept answers indicating an understanding of the importance of prayer, worship, praise, and service in the lives of believers.
5. Answers should indicate an understanding of the importance of learning God's Word.

Writing:

. *Optional— This activity can be completed by letting children work in pairs or small groups of three or four.

May

Questions:

1. Jabu learned the 23rd Psalm.
2. Yes. He remembered God was with him.
3. He felt better knowing he was not alone.
4. Accept answers such as God is faithful, we can depend on God,
   God hears our prayers, we don't have to be afraid.

Writing:

1. Encourage students to share their prayer.

June

Questions:

1. Corrine was afraid to enter because she didn't know anyone.
2. Answers will vary.
3. She saw that the teacher and the students were smiling.
4. Yes. She felt welcomed by the teacher and students.

Writing:

1. Let volunteers share their cards by reading them aloud.
*Display cards on a bulletin board if available.

July

Questions:

1. She sewed beautiful pillows.
2. She wanted to pass the craft of sewing down to Amahle.
3. Probably. She was very eager to learn and seemed to enjoy it.
4. **Answers will vary.** Acceptable responses: knowledge about Jesus,
   musical abilities, kindness to others, etc.

Writing:

Correct order of answers:

1. Way— **Direction**
2. Turn—**Change direction**
3. Mercy—**Compassion**
4. Start—**Beginning**
5. Path—**Route**
6. Right—**Correct**

*Sentences will vary   (Puzzle solution- p. 86)

August

Questions:

1. She didn't look like the girl on the magazine cover.
2. Answers will vary.
3. Answers will vary.
4. Answers will vary (**acceptable answers**: God's Word says I am special, valuable, loved, God's child, etc.

Writing:

Learning about Jesus makes me feel: (acceptable answers could be: loved, like I am His child,
valuable, special, etc.)

September

Questions:

1. No. Elizabeth's behavior was selfish.
2. It means to be modest; not bragging about ones abilities.
3. Yes. We are to imitate Jesus's behavior.
4. Being insensitive to others, bragging, and selfish behavior
5. Answers will vary: (examples such as good, wonderful, better are   .
   acceptable).

Writing:
Poem completion should center on the idea of being humble and helping others.
*Encourage children to share their completed poem.

October

Questions:

1. They were afraid because of the storm.
2. No. Mother and Father believed they would all be protected.
3. He believed God would hear his prayer and watch over his family.
4. Answers will vary (encourage children to trust that God hears their prayers).
5. No. God hears every prayer.

Writing: Students should have circled the following words:
Brave Hero Listener Defender Champion Guardian Savior
Shield Guard Friend Helper Conqueror Victor Warrior
. Supporter Advocate

November

Questions:

1. Faith was nervous about the tryouts. She probably knew she didn't sing well.
2. Answers will vary.
3. Yes. Mrs. James told Faith God wants every voice to
   Give Him praise.
4. Answers will vary. (answers should be supported with evidence
   inferred from the story.

Writing: Unscramble the words.
Children   Praise   Stronghold
Infants Enemies   foe silence

December

Questions:

1. Trey liked living with the Allens and he knew he would probably be leaving soon.
2. Yes. Michael was concerned that Trey was upset.
3. He loved them all.
4. Happy. Mr. and Mrs. Allen probably would not have considered adoption if the children didn't get along.

Writing:
Sentence: I have been adopted into God's family.

Word Search solution

A Good Start

```
h g n h w f n r d c c c z r v
P b o b y c v r l l u d n a k
h e k z z n o t u c u l o v e
g g e t r v h m h t t o s i k
g i m b j g f i p o h w h n t
n n l l i w l i n a a e w s r
e n n r h d i a g y s h y u a
v i f o r g i v e n e s s c t
e n f e m o s s e n d n i k s
n g n q o i f t d q t e n o h
z r e e r r e h f l a h x r y n
d n l q f t r m o d e c w a c
s g a e a e e o z w w g p y b
y i x p d a g p q t l i w f y
m e r c y f l e i u s l j b w
```

90

Other Books
By Mabel Elizabeth Singletary

1. *Just Jump!*
   ISBN: 978-0-8024-2251-4

2. *Something To Jump About*
   ISBN: 978-0-8024-2252-1

3. *A Promise and a Rainbow*
   ISBN: 978-0-8024-2255-2

4. *Run, Jeremiah Run!*
   ISBN: 978-0-8024-2253-8

5. *Coming Across Jordan*
   ISBN: 978-0-8024-2259-0

6. *Leon's Share*
   ISBN: 978-0-9886553-0-0

7. *Leon's Share: Question &*
   Answer   Activity Book
   ISBN: 9780988655317

8. *Finding Alan Treadwell*
   ISBN: 9780988655324

*Available at: MightyWaybooks.com, Ingram Distributing,
Barnesandnoble.com, Booksamillion.com & Amazon.com*

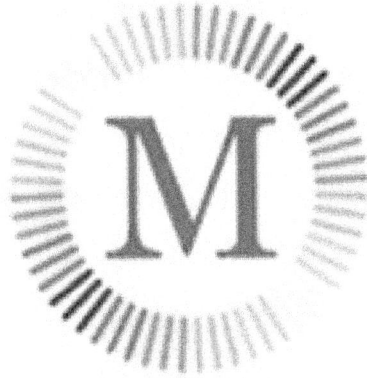

MightyWayBooks

"Encouraging children one story at a time"

www.mightywaybooks.com

www.ingramcontent.com/pod-product-compliance
Lightning Source LLC
Chambersburg PA
CBHW081518040426
42447CB00013B/3260